Bear Hollow Tales

Also by Forrest Alford

Strange But True! Tokens, Floating Blue Lights and Ghostly Figures

BEAR HOLLOW TALES

Forrest Alford

PUBLISHING

ISBN-13: 978-0-9801862-5-3

Printed in the United States of America

Published by:

Wythe-North Publishing
PO Box 1208
Proctorville, Ohio 45669

www.wythe-north.com

Dedication

To my children:
Veronica, Brad, Rick and Freda

Acknowledgement

I wish to thank our dear friend, Peggy Crutchfield, for what she means to our family, and for her encouragement as I was writing the book and for proofing it and typing it for me—and for leaving the stories as I wrote them.

Table of Contents

Foreword

My name is Forrest Alford. I was born and raised in Mason County, West Virginia, in the year 1936, near the Mason–Cabell line.

Times were hard as we had to work and help out with the farming and gardens that we always had. We always had plenty to eat, and never had to go to bed hungry. My Dad worked for the railroad and was away all week in Raleigh County, but was home most weekends. When I was a baby, he gave me the nickname "Cock Robin" and it has stuck with me. My Mom was a good and kind woman. She always looked out for the ones in the community that were less fortunate than we were. There were fourteen of us children with quite a bit of years between the oldest to the youngest. (I had nephews and nieces older than me.) Nine boys and five girls total, me being a seventh son.

Now, everyone knows Number Seven is a lucky number and I look back on my life and I am 100% sure of that. I have been blessed all of my life.

My family was quite a bunch of readers when I was a kid. If they got hold of a book or a newspaper, they would read it from cover to cover as they sat by the Kerosene lamps each night, but when daylight came, there was work to be done—and we did it, from the oldest to the youngest.

As I grew older, in my early teens, I was the oldest one at home at that time. I had to do a man's job from the time I was thirteen. I never got to be a boy—just a young man.

About that time of my life, I started night hunting for opossums and coons. I loved to night hunt. Many times, I went hunting by myself, as my two brothers, Herbert and Wendell, who were home at that time, had no interest in night hunting. I hunted by myself and sometimes I would have a friend or two that would go with me.

Now most of the stories that I have written took place in and around Mason County, or are about people born in the area, and most came about after I was married with a family. Some you will find hard to believe but they are true. Man has a tendency to only believe what he can see for himself. I know that some of the most powerful forces on earth cannot be seen with the naked eye, such as the atom, and wind, for example. We have both of them on earth, as we do the strange life and ghostly images that I have written about. The stories are true, believe them or not. This book is a follow-up to my previous book, *Strange But True.*

I am now seventy-three years old and wanted to pass along some of life's experiences before I am called home with friends and loved ones and my Savior, JESUS CHRIST!

The Indian Brave

This story took place about thirty years ago. Sean himself told it to me.

Sean's dad David and mother Bonnie lived in Milton, West Virginia, on Second Street. They were good Christian folks and hard workers. No better young people could be found. They taught their children to always tell the truth, no matter what.

Sean was in first grade at the time, and one day he was playing with some dominoes on their front porch. He looked out toward the street, and to his surprise, there sat an Indian brave on his pony. He had his face painted and a full headdress of feathers on his head. They were something breathtaking—bright and shiny. The Indian stared at Sean for a while and the pony never moved, standing with his head up as the Indian sat erect and was not using a saddle.

Sean, not believing what he was seeing, ran in the house to get his mother. He was plenty excited as he told her what he had seen. She came running to see for herself. When she got to the porch and looked out at the street, nothing was there. She scolded Sean about his Indian story, telling him not to make up stories.

Sean was about six years old at the time that he saw the Indian. He is now in his thirties and tells the story with vivid descriptions. He said the sighting is true and he will never forget what he saw and that it is not made up.

Now and then he drives his car down Second Street. He always looks to see if he can see the brave and his pony. He has never seen it again but no one can take this beautiful memory from him. Sean is a college graduate and is a very nice person with children of his own. I'm sure the children will hear this story many times.

Rick's Light

Rick told me this story that happened on Rocky Fork in Mason County, West Virginia.

It was late fall on a very nice warm night. It was quiet and peaceful as he stepped outside the house. He was ready for bed and just wanted to enjoy the nice warm air before retiring.

All at once he saw a round light coming over the hill about the size of a No. 3 washtub or approximately three and one-half by two and one-half feet. As the light got over his head, he never heard a sound of any kind. He said it felt as though the air was sucked out from around him and the leaves on the trees were standing straight up. He watched the light for a few minutes as it went over his head and on up the hollow. He decided he would walk up the road a piece to see what the light was doing. As he walked a few feet, he saw the light come down in a field not more than fifty yards away.

The clouds covered the moon a few minutes as Rick stood looking at the field. The moon came out from behind the clouds—it was almost as light as day. Nothing could be seen in the field except grass.

What caused the light that sucked the air up, making the leaves stand, but made no sound, and could not be seen after it came to the ground?

I guess we will never know these strange but true happenings.

Preacher Hudson

The events of Preacher Hudson's death were told to me by his son.

I first met preacher Hudson back in 1969. He was a first class gentleman—none better. He also was a little long-winded sometimes as he brought his message in Church.

One day his sermon was on praying. He told of a man that always had to out-pray all the rest of the congregation. He would go on for some time, a lot longer than necessary.

One day Preacher Hudson decided to break him of this, so during the service he called on the brother to pray. He prayed a very long prayer as usual. They all sang a song and the Preacher called on the same man to pray again. He prayed his usual long prayer but managed to cut it shorter. After another song, Preacher Hudson called on the same man to pray again. This time, he cut the prayer much shorter. The same thing continued until the man got the message and his last prayer was short and sweet. After Church, he asked the Preacher why he was called on to pray so many times. Preacher Hudson replied, "If you will pray more during the week, you won't have to pray so much on Sundays."

Now on the way home from Church that morning,

my youngest son, Rick (who was five at the time and quite witty), had this to say: "I wish Preacher Hudson would preach more during the week so he wouldn't preach so long on Sunday." We all got a kick out of that.

We were able to hunt and visit a lot with the family in West Virginia. He loved the mountains of West Virginia. I'm sure he felt it a spiritual place to be. He especially was fond of the valley between Marlinton and Dunmore.

Later on, Preacher Hudson moved his family back to Missouri. He preached there until his death. We were able to visit them and they would come here to visit us. He loved to eat at our house. He was a good, kind-hearted man. He helped anyone he could, which was many.

He took sick in his eighties and had to go to the hospital. His time had come to leave this world. His children were called in to see their Dad for the last time. His wife Bessie stayed outside his room so the kids could tell their Dad goodbye.

After the kids left, Bessie went in to say her goodbye to him. He told her he loved her very much but that he had to go with the two men in white that had come to take him.

They were telling her to say goodbye first. She could not see them and asked where they were. He said, "Can't you see them by the door?"

Bessie said, "There is no one there that I can see."

She bent over and kissed him for the last time and went out to get the children After a few minutes, they came back in the room, only to find him dead. The two angels in white had taken him home.

Rap on the Wall

This is a true story about my oldest brother, Tom. Tom loved teasing people, especially small children.

I worked a lot of days for Tom on his farm. He always paid me well for the work I helped him do. He treated me more like a son than a brother. We hunted, fished and worked together, never having any angry words.

There are many things I could write about Tom to tell what a good hunter and farmer he was. He always had the biggest tobacco, the best milk cows, and killed more rabbits and squirrels than anyone else. He was good at what he did. As years went by, I grew up, got married, and had a family of my own.

Tom's health began to fail in his fifties. He had several heart attacks and was a diabetic, and it all took its toll on his mind before he died. My wife Stella and I were there with his family the day he took his last breath. A very sad day to say the least.

Tom's wife, and now widow, told Stella and I many times that she saw Tom standing in the bedroom near where a chest of drawers stood. We thought she may have imagined it until one night we were there to visit her.

It was a cold night and the snow was falling quite hard.

When we went in the house was hot and as we sat talking, the longer we sat there, the hotter it got, so I moved over near the door. The house had four windows side by side at the end where I was sitting.

As we talked, the three of us heard a loud *Rap! Rap! Rap!* on the wall near the window. Thinking someone was at the door, I got up to let them in. When I opened the door, no one was there. I sat back down to chat a little more and Lucy said it might be a neighbor's children trying to scare her.

After about five minutes, we heard the *Rap! Rap! Rap!* again. I jumped up as fast as I could and opened the door, trying to catch the one doing the rapping; but again, no one was there. This time I went outside looking for tracks in the snow but none were found. I went all around the house but no tracks could be found.

Later, Lucy said she never heard the rapping again. She said Tom appeared to her one night and told her not to worry about him, that he was in Heaven and okay. She also said she was wide awake when she saw him.

Lucy soon moved and the farmhouse has been torn down and a housing development is on the farm he loved. I still wonder about the rapping I heard on the wall.

The Wedding

This story was told to me by a woman that said it was as true as could be.

She said that she knew a woman that had picked up a ghost one day and that she was with her the day it happened.

It seems that a young couple was going to get married. The young girl was at the Church, waiting for her lover to show up. He was late and that was something he never did. He was always on time all but this once.

A young man came running up to the young girl's dad, saying he needed to talk with him in private. The young girl's dad stepped outside to see what the young man had to say. The tale he was to hear was one that no one wants to hear if he loves his girls as this man did.

His daughter's boyfriend had been run over by a big earthmover that was working on a new road being built. He was killed on the way to the wedding.

The young bride-to-be soon was told the same story. She could not stand the pain so she ran from the Church and jumped in her car, giving it too much gas. She lost control of her car, hit a tree, and was killed. She never got to the place her lover died, but she died trying.

As years passed, on the very same day each year that the wedding was to have taken place, it has been said that a young woman in a white wedding gown can be seen walking the road where the young bride-to-be had died.

As the woman told me about the story, she said, "This is the part you probably won't believe." She said that she and her girl friends were on their way to a school dance in an old station wagon when they saw a young woman walking by the road where the young girl had died. She said that they stopped to see if the girl in the white gown wanted to ride. She said the young girl got in the back seat, not saying anything at all.

She said that she and her girl friends were singing and acting up as young girls do sometimes. As they pulled into the parking lot, they got out of the car. No one could get out unless the car was stopped but the girl in white did. She was nowhere to be seen. She had just vanished.

I asked the woman that told me the story if she and her friends were drinking. She said that she and her friends didn't drink. They were just teenage girls trying to do a young girl a favor by giving her a ride that neither will ever forget.

The Ghost That Wasn't

Back in the year 1957 (the year my Mom died), my wife and I moved in with my Dad to help him out with the farm. We stayed with him about eight months. I was laid off from work as things were slow at the time and not much work could be found around this part of the country.

My Dad and I decided to raise five crops of tobacco. I rented two crops and my Dad had three. I sure had a hard time that summer.

One of the tobacco crops I rented was about two miles down the hollow from our old home place. The farm had an old house and a barn. A lot of people said that the old Price house was haunted. I never did believe it.

One day I had the horses down there disking the tobacco field. It was just in front of the house. All at once I heard a very loud rumble in the house. It scared the horses as I was turning them around in front of the old house. I got them calmed down after a little bit. Not knowing what had made the noise, I got me a hammer from the toolbox on the disk and went up to the house to see what had made that racket.

I didn't walk very fast as I was a little bit scared. In fact, I was a whole lot scared. Just as I reached the front porch, a big white-faced bull stuck his head out of one of the windows. He had entered the house from the back door.

I was always afraid of bulls but this time it sure looked good to me. I ran the bull out of the house, then shut the back door so he could not get back in.

That was the last time anyone ever heard the loud thumping in the house.

That was one time I sure was glad to see a bull.

Some ghostly sounds can be found to just be something that can be figured out—like the bull.

Then again, some cannot be explained.

The Big Rock Cliff

Who was that woman that lost her life that night when her horse ran over the cliff?

This took place a very long time ago. My Grandpa knew the woman and her family very well.

As time has a way of changing things, it sure did a good job with this woman's name. No one can remember much about her—only that she died a very frightful death.

It has been said that one night she was going home from a friend's house. It was very dark—a storm was coming fast and she had to go across a hollow known as Hell Hollow.

The hollow got the name Hell Hollow because it was always hot. Old timers said it was hot as Hell—therefore the name Hell Hollow. That is what the hollow is called to this day.

As the woman was coming along the ridge top, lightning struck a tree near the top of the hill that scared the horse. It started to run as fast as it could down the hill toward a very tall rock cliff that was in a curve of the road. The road was near the top of the rock. As the horse was running full speed when it came to the curve, the buggy it was pulling with the woman inside slipped over the cliff, pulling the horse with it as it went, killing the woman and her horse.

They were found the next day.

As time went on, people said that on dark stormy nights, you could hear a woman scream if you were near the rock cliff. Some say you can hear the horse screaming its death scream also.

The Small Light and Slippers

Back about twenty-five years ago, this young boy and his father shared the same bedroom in the house where they lived. The young boy's dad and mother had divorced, leaving the young man to raise his son. The young man's dad let the two of them live in a small house that he and his wife owned.

This is the story as it was told to me by the two of them.

The young boy said that sometimes while he was at the table eating, he would see a pair of white slippers near the kitchen in the hallway. They would be there for just a few seconds and then disappear. He said that he had seen the white slippers many times while eating at the table.

His dad told me about a small red light about the size of a dime that he and his son had seen many times in their bedroom. He said the light would be on the bedroom wall about halfway up. The first time they saw the light, they thought it might just be a reflection from something shining through the windows, but each time, the small light appeared, it was brighter than the last time. It was now about the size of a golf ball.

One day, the young man said that he went in the bedroom before he and his son went to bed and placed

15

very dark curtains on the windows so no light at all would shine in. That night, at about three a.m., the light appeared on the wall making its way around the room as usual. This went on for as long as they lived in the house. He said that he had seen a shadow-like form a few times, going from the living room to the hallway. Also they would hear a door slam shut, only to find someone had shut or opened it.

Upon checking around about the old house, he found out that a man had died there in years past and that the old man was an early riser. He was up at three a.m. every morning—the same time the red light would appear on the wall.

Were the white slippers and the red light the old man's spirit still in the house that he had lived in until his death?

The young boy and his dad moved from the house soon after they found out about the old man.

Time goes on. The young man is now twenty-eight years old, living alone. He still visits the old house now and then but has not seen the slippers or the red light for years.

I guess the old man's spirit is at rest, at least I hope so.

After writing this story, I was telling my wife about writing it. We now live in the old house. Just as I finished telling her about it, we both heard a door shut in the hallway. I got up to check it out, only to find that all the doors that lead to the bedrooms and bathroom standing wide open, Didn't scare me much.

I guess he is still there.

The Small Jets—or UFOs?

A very good friend of mine, who I will just call Papa, told me this strange tale. He is a truthful man and not one to make things up. He is also quite a hunter. He really looks forward to deer hunting season every year. He said he would tell me something if I promised not to think he was crazy. I promised I would not, so he told me of his early morning deer hunt about twenty years ago.

It was getting pretty light outside, as he had just climbed a hill on a farm in Mason County. As he reached the top of the hill there was a very nice flat field about forty yards wide. There was a row of pines on the opposite side of the field where he was standing. The pines had about five strands of barbed wire nailed on them as they were used for fence posts for someone's pasture.

As Papa was crossing the field he saw three small jets around two feet long fly over his head, making no noise at all. As they went over the pines, they made a nose dive straight down. They were so small for jets and not flying very high, about two hundred feet at the highest point.

When the tiny jets made the nosedive, Papa was sure he was going to hear some loud noise of the jets crashing, but he never heard a sound. Thinking this to be quite strange, he walked over to the pine trees to have a look. All he saw was a large lake about five acres in size below him on the other side of the mountain. He said there was never any sound and no way the jets could be anywhere except in the lake.

He found a good spot overlooking the flat field and lake. He sat down to watch for deer and the lake. Seeing no deer or jets, he started home around noon. As he was walking back to his truck, a thought came to him that if some alien were to pay a visit to Earth, where would be a better place to hide than in the water?

Could it be that was what happened that morning? No one knows.

The Chasing Light

Back in the 1960s, a lot of folks around here told of seeing lights or UFOs.

This happening was told to me by a very good friend of mine—I will just call him Everett.

Everett had a younger sister that worked the evening shift at a fast food place near Barboursville, West Virginia.

One night she was going from work to her home in Milton, about twelve miles from the job. There wasn't near as much traffic back then as there is now. Sometimes she could drive from her workplace to her home without meeting one car.

As she was driving up Route 60, she noticed a light moving the same way she was going. It was moving at a very slow speed. She thought this was quite strange. It followed her all the way to the old tin bridge west of the town of Milton, where it disappeared.

Everett said when his sister got home, she told of the light she had seen. Her dad and mother knew she wasn't making it up, because when she told you something you could trust her.

Her dad was quite concerned and told her to be very careful when coming home

The next night, as she was going home, she said the light appeared again, only this time it was much closer than it had been the night before. She was very scared and she gave the car the gas to outrun the light. That didn't work. It came right over her car and lowered to about fifty feet over her car. She described it as six feet wide with a dull glow about it. The light stayed just over top of her car until she reached the old tin bridge again. The light just vanished from sight. This was the last time she ever saw the light.

Every night after work, as she drove home, she always looked to see if she was being followed by the light. She never was.

No one ever knew what the light was, so they just called it a UFO.

Marty's Mom

Marty is a very good friend of ours that lives nearby. You could not ask for a better neighbor. He read my first book *Strange But True* and said he enjoyed it. He called his Mom and was telling her about the book and told her he had a neighbor about three-quarters of a bubble off. She asked why was he saying this about this neighbor as she knew we had been close friends. Marty replied, "It's this book he wrote about strange lights and other things." His Mother said if everyone that has seen these lights is crazy, then so am I. She went on to tell him about her seeing strange lights.

When she was a young girl they had no electricity, only lamp lights. There was an old house down the road from where she lived that an old couple had lived in for years. When the old man died, his wife went to live with her sister in a small town in West Virginia, never to see the old house again. Marty's Mom and her older sister were playing on their front porch after the old man had died. They looked down the street to the old house and saw a light inside. Not a bright light but light enough to tell something was going on. She ran in the house to tell her Dad and brother about the light and the Dad and brother left to go see what was going on. As they drew closer to the house, they could see lights near the windows. Both lights were about basketball size and blue in color.

When the Dad and brother got within fifty feet of the lights, they both went out at the same time. Her Dad and brother checked the house—all doors and windows were locked. No one could be found. No tracks, or anything. Being quite puzzled, they walked back home. About a week later, Marty's Mom and her sister saw the lights again. They ran to tell their Dad about the blue lights they had seen. Only one light this time, not two, as before. Her Dad came to the porch to see the light and could see it. He said, "I am not going to go back down there again." When they asked him why, he said, "There is something strange about the blue lights." After hearing his Mother tell about the lights, he came back and bought four more of my books for his friends.

Burning of the Old Home Place

As I wrote in my earlier book *Strange But True*, this story is the end of a long list of sightings of a blue light.

The people that bought the old home place I called home for twenty years, let the old house go to pieces. A storm had blown part of the roof off, leaving a gaping hole for rain, snow and varmints to come in.

The blue light had been seen a few times near the old house. Just to be on the safe side, they never went around it much.

One day, the man's son (who now owned the place as his mom and dad had passed on) decided it was time to get rid of the old house once and for all. The Fire Department gave them permission to burn the house down, and he did just that.

It was a sad day for my two younger brothers and I. We grew up in that old house. We never looked at it as being just a house. We saw it as a home. The best home money could buy.

As I look back at the good times we had when our mom was living, at times it is hard to keep the tears back. Our dad worked away during the week. He would come home on Sundays, leave on Monday, with orders as to what work he wanted done each week. My two younger brothers and I always finished the jobs before he came home. He always had us another list to do the following week. This continued until I left home.

The old place started to look bad. Brush soon took over the pasture fields we had kept looking so good. I learned a lesson back then—it is so much easier to give out job lists than it is to do them.

After the burning of the old home place, all that is left are some pictures of the old home place that I have hanging on my bedroom wall.

It has been ten years or so since the house was burned. I have walked down many times to reminisce and to coon hunt in the place I always loved to hunt.

Never once have I seen the blue light again. As far as I know, no one else has seen the blue light again.

I guess the blue light went out the day the old house was burned—never to be seen again.

Little Seven-Mile Soldier

This tale was told to me by a very good friend of mine. He was raised on Little Seven-Mile Creek located about seven miles north of Huntington, West Virginia, off Route 2.

The war was going on. The year was 1941.

A young man came home on leave before he was to be sent to Germany to fight for his country. He had a few dollars in his pocket at the time but soon had more as he was a good card player. His skill with cards is what got him killed.

There were two women that lived on Little Seven-Mile at the time that had seen the young man win a few card games. He had a few dollars in his pocket and they wanted the money.

One of the women, who was about twenty at the time, came up with a scheme to relieve the young many of his money.

She and her mother invited the young man over one night before he was to leave, telling the young soldier they wanted to fix him a good meal before he left.

The young man thought that was so nice of them and told his mother about the two women. He gave his mother a kiss on the cheek, saying he would be back about nine o'clock. He never showed up at home again.

As he was eating the supper the two women had fixed for him, one of the women took a hammer and struck him from behind, killing him, as he took the last bite of food in his life.

The women took his money from him. Not being strong enough to drag his body to the creek as they had planned, they put his body under the front porch steps, covering it with dirt the best they could.

When the young man didn't come home as he had promised, his mother asked around the neighborhood if anyone had seen him. No one had, so she called the police. After a very short search, the body was found when a dog was seen digging by the front step, exposing the young man's uniform.

The two women were tried and convicted of his murder. They spent the rest of their days in the penitentiary.

Soon after the murder of the soldier, it was said that on some nights if you were in front of the house, you could hear someone dragging the soldier to the door, then down the steps.

It has been said that you could see the front door open on the old house, and then hear the soldier's feet hit the seven steps as he was being dragged down them.

This went on for years. No one would live in the old house after that. It stood empty for years before it was torn down and burned.

There is now a trailer on the place the old house sat. No one hears anything anymore. I guess the young soldier is at rest with his mother. I hope so anyway.

Is He Still There?

This is about a very good man—a truthful person. This is how the story came about.

Back in the early fifties, there lived an older couple, George and Vada. They were very well liked in the community. As a young man, I would stop at times to chat a bit with them. I most always made it about suppertime. Vada was a very good cook and always made me feel welcome. They were my dearest friends.

Now, time has a way of changing things. George and Vada had grown old and had to sell their farm. I will never forget how bad I felt when they left the farm that they sold to Mr. K. Mr. K. had a wife and two small children that were staying until the children finished Elementary school.

Mr. K. lived alone for quite some time. We became good friends and had many long talks about farming. I knew a little about farming as I was in high school and Future Farmers of America was one of my best subjects.

Mr. K. was from the city and knew nothing about farming. He bought a tractor and equipment and was ready to give it a try. He built a nice brick house that anyone would love. One day he did not come out of the house. He was found dead in bed. His wife and son lived there for some time, not fixing the place up, just junking it up.

Soon the son took sick and passed away. Now Mrs. K. had to sell the farm because she could not take care of it. She sold it to my now good friend J.N. When Mr. J.N. took the place over, he soon had it looking like a picture. He and his sons worked very hard and it showed. He likes to work his tractor and loves his riding horses.

One day J.N. was out back working and he heard someone say something not in plain English. That is how Mr. K. talked as he was from another country other than the United States. He dismissed the encounter and went on with his work. Soon after he heard the muffled broken English voice again. Not wanting to scare his wife, he said nothing about it.

While visiting me one day, he told me about it. I was quite puzzled when he spoke of the broken English.

After a while, J.N. started seeing a shadow-like form going from the room he uses as a living room. His wife has seen the shadow-like form of a short heavyset man like Mr. K. was.

Now I wonder: is Mr. K.'s spirit still around? What else could it be?

I'll bet if it is Mr. K.'s spirit, it is well pleased with the way J.N. has fixed up the place. The house is always spotless and the rest of the farm is a picture to see.

Trail's End is name of the farm.

Green Meadows Ghost

Back in the late thirties and early forties here in West Virginia, times were hard. Many people had a very hard time feeding their families. Most raised about all of their food, working from sunup until dark. Just as it is today, some didn't like to work all day long. They liked to sleep during the day and stay up all night making moonshine, selling it for a profit, and not caring who they hurt along the way. Many men got hooked on moonshine, ending up with nothing in this life but misery, that being the case of Green Meadows.

Green was a big man—short and stocky. He had a very big drinking problem. Every man around feared Green when he was drinking, as he could get very mean. Not many wanted anything to do with him.

In the year 1946, I was eleven years old—not old enough to know how to strip tobacco. We hired Green to strip the tobacco for us that year. He taught me how to do it so I could do it the next year myself.

It took about a week to strip what tobacco we had that year. We all enjoyed working with him, as he had a lot of stories to tell us kids. He was a perfect gentleman.

It was a sad day for us when he finished the tobacco that year, as we watched him go up the hill in front of our old home place for the last time.

It was about two years later that we heard that Green had been killed. Someone shot him in the house he lived in, leaving the gun on the front door step. Green was found on his bed that was about thirty feet from the front door. He had a bullet hole between his eyes.

The Sheriff said that he had killed himself— we have always had that kind of sheriff here—not knowing how to solve a three-piece jigsaw puzzle.

The old house that Green lived in stood empty for years. Around 1980, a family moved in the old house. They didn't stay long, saying that the place was haunted, so once again, the place was left empty.

It stood empty for about ten years until another man moved in. That didn't last long. The man's wife said that every time she was alone in the house, she would see a shadow-like form cross the room. Also, she would hear footsteps sometimes but no one would be there.

The woman would tell her husband about it and he would just laugh at her.

She had all of this she could stand, living alone all week, while her husband worked away, coming home on weekends.

The man had a vacation week coming to him about the time his wife left him. Being alone one night was enough for him. He moved out the next day.

Now, the question is: what had he seen or heard that caused him to leave so soon? He wouldn't say.

Is Green's spirit still in the old house? If not, what is?

The Old Post Office

Years ago, my Grandfather worked as a mail carrier; he was also a Preacher. The two jobs kept him busy.

Here in West Virginia, you have to be a Democrat to get a job carrying the mail. My Granddad didn't pass his beliefs on to me. I like to use a little common sense and vote for the best man. Most of the time I lose my vote. I have always been a loser, so it doesn't matter anyway.

The old Post Office sat upon a hill above where my Grandpa lived. He rode his horse to carry the mail back in those days, the late 1800s.

Most all of the houses back then didn't have paint on them. People didn't have the money to paint them like they would like to.

The old Post Office was an exception. It was painted white. We all called it "the white house."

After my Granddad died, the Post Office was moved to Milton, leaving the house empty for many years, It was soon purchased by a man whose name was White. He owned the place for years, only living in the house a very short time. He moved out, leaving the house empty for years. It was always known as the "old white house" by all of us at home.

Our place joined the White place. We hunted the

31

place for small game just like we owned it. All Mr. White said was that he wanted us to keep a watch out for him, making sure no fires were to be set.

The old house was a very sad looking place. It sat back in the pines off a small road that lead to a couple of farms past it.

One day my brother said he wanted to go hunting up on the old White place, asking if I would like to go. Being a young boy of about eight, I was ready in a flash.

When we got to the old White house, it was not quite time for the squirrels to come out. We decided to take a look inside the old house. The house had an upstairs in it. The steps were as strong as the rest of the house. Not being afraid of the steps to the upstairs falling, we went up to have a look around. The upstairs was very dusty. You could see squirrel tracks in the dust. There was another track leading over to the window. It was a very muddy track of a man's footprint. The mud was fresh. How could that be, we hadn't had a rain in weeks?

We got an old broom and swept the muddy tracks down the steps before we left the old house.

About a week later, my brother wanted to go hunting again, asking if I would go with him. Now, as I look back, I think he was afraid to hunt on the old White place alone.

So away we went, back to the old White house, as before.

When we went into the old house, there weren't any tracks at all downstairs or on the steps. When we got upstairs, there to our surprise, were the same muddy footprints again. It was drier then, as we hadn't had a drop of rain for six weeks. We swept the tracks out again before leaving.

I didn't go back in the old house for years after that. Being a man about eighteen years old, I decided to look the old house over again. Reaching the upstairs, much to my surprise, I found the same muddy tracks again—with fresh mud, as before.

A man bought the old White place about a year later. He decided the house was too old and in much need of extensive repair, so he decided to tear the place down.

After the place the old house stood on was cleaned up, it looked good for about a week. Then, much to everyone's surprise, a fresh water spring started flowing on top of the ground where the house had been standing, high on the very top of a hill.

The fresh water spring is flowing as of this day, forty years from the time it first started to put forth the fresh water that flows from its vein that was under the old White House Post Office.

The Floating Woman

Back in the early 1940s, it was not unusual to hear of ghosts as almost everyone back then died at home. Some say people's spirits stayed on some time before moving on. Also, some people would lose their lives due to some accident or maybe someone would end their life with a gun or knife.

These sightings always took place in the same area just past our neighbor's house. I will just call him C.H.

Not everyone saw the woman that was said to just float about ten feet above the ground, but a lot of people said they saw her.

This continued for years. The road was always bad at this spot. There was a sharp curve at the top of a small hill where some say a woman lost her life when the buggy she was riding turned over. She was going too fast to make the turn in the curve. I guess women haven't changed much as most of them still go too fast; they probably always will.

About 1949, the State Road commission decided to take out the sharp curve, which they did. It is now a long sweeping curve.

About ten years ago, a black man, not knowing the curve, came around it too fast and lost control of his car. He hit a tree and was killed instantly. Ever since the state changed the road, the floating woman has not been seen.

About five years ago, a woman and her two children came around the curve on their way to town. The woman hit the same tree that the black man hit. She was wearing her seat belt and so were the children. They were not hurt much.

When the Sheriff arrived on the scene, he asked the woman what caused her to leave the road. She said she swerved to keep from hitting a man standing in the road in her lane. She asked the Sheriff if the man was okay. The Sheriff assured her that no one was to be found at the scene but her and the two children.

Now people are saying that if you are walking the road in late summer or early fall, when you reach the tree standing by the road where the man was killed and the woman wrecked, that you can small fruit very strong.

There hasn't been any fruit grown near the spot of the accident for years.

Speaking for myself, I never walk the road anymore. I always drive my truck. But, I do take a good hard sniff as I drive by. Up to this date, I haven't smelled anything, but who am I to say they are not telling the truth? (I wonder!)

The Crab Creek Ghost

Crab Creek is a long creek that runs into the Ohio River about five miles south of Point Pleasant, West Virginia.

Point Pleasant is the county seat of Mason County, which is famous for the Indian War with Cornstalk and the Mothman. The Mothman was seen by a lot of folks about the time the Silver Bridge fell into the Ohio River, killing some of the people that were crossing it when it fell.

It has often been said that Chief Cornstalk placed a curse on the town. A lot of people around the little town believe that he did. I could write a lot of tales about Point Pleasant, as many people have told stories about seeing ghostly forms of Indians and so on.

This Crab Creek Ghost story was told to me by a very good Christian woman that is a member of the church my youngest daughter attends. Here is the story as it was told to me by Frankie B.

"When I first saw our home in the country, I knew this was where our family was supposed to live. I had prayed to God that I wanted a white house with enough land to plant a garden and to have flowers all around the house.

"Part of the house was close to two hundred years

old. It was a two-story structure made of large logs. Part of the house was only about ten years old. Our second child was born after we moved in. It was June 1980 when we moved and she was born in September. Being on a tight budget, we could only do fix-up as we got the money. We finally built a two-car garage detached from the house. Many a time, I would be home by myself and would hear a door shut and I would get up and go to the front door, thinking my husband was home, but no one was outside. I would walk to the door and it would be shut tight.

Several years passed and my father died and left me some money, so we tore down the old kitchen, which we never used, and built a large new living room with another bathroom and laundry room.

One night after we moved our living room into this new room, I was watching TV and a white figure of a woman walked past the door and upstairs to our girls' bedrooms. My husband and girls were not at home at the time, so when they came home, I told them what I saw. Of course they laughed at me until one night my older daughter and my younger daughter saw the white figure walk past the door and go upstairs. We never felt any fears. I felt since it was white, it was some form of an Angel.

My husband was always afraid to be at the house by himself, but I never felt any fear being in the house. We recently moved to town, and I hope the new owners have an encounter like we did.

It was told that an Indian woman was killed in the house and it could be her roaming in and out of the house.

The Eggins House

Back in the early forties, the depression had ended for most folks, but not all. Many people had moved to the cities to find work, only to leave the houses they had lived in empty. You could find empty houses everywhere. The old farms were growing up fast. Some of the farms were left abandoned by the owners who had farmed there until the day they died. This was the case of the Eggins place.

The old house stood empty for years. The land soon grew up with pine trees and brush. People would joke and say that brush, broom sage and Chapmans had taken the county over. A lot of Chapmans lived in the community.

The pines grew fast and tall, making a place for young men and women to go and do whatever. It has been said Goodyear got its start here.

There was one man by the name of Harvey who had a farm not very far from the Eggin's place which he farmed for a living. He had a houseful of children. When they stood in line to have a picture taken, it looked like a big long stair step. Harvey had a hard time trying to feed his large family. His wife worked hard also. There was a lot of small game back then to help feed the people.

I think God has always taken care of us. He

provides us with our every need. Back in the forties we sure did need the squirrels and rabbits to eat. A groundhog now and then didn't hurt much. They were very good to eat if cooked right.

The winter of 1943 was very cold. We had some very big snows that year. The tobacco everyone grew back then was sold to help pay the taxes and grocery bills. The tobacco was all stripped and sold from Harvey's farm, leaving nothing to do but hunt for some small game.

One day, Harvey decided he would kill a few rabbits for supper. The old Eggins place was full of rabbits and squirrels. On this particular day, there was a big snow, making it easy to track a rabbit to his hiding place. Harvey was a good rabbit tracker. He walked up toward the old Eggins house thinking, "Not a rabbit track in sight." As he walked around back of the old house, he found some fresh tracks, not a rabbit, but a man's tracks. The tracks only went out about ten feet, then back to the house again. Harvey, not being afraid of anything, went in the old house to see who it was that had made the tracks.

The house was empty—nothing but four walls. All five rooms were the same. There was no place for anyone to hide. Harvey went back outside and the only track he saw was his own. No one had left the house.

It had been told around that the house was haunted. Harvey, not being sure of this, decided he no longer wanted rabbit for supper. He left the old home in a flash.

Winter was soon gone. Spring was here—in fact, a very wet spring.

The war was going on in the year 1943. Almost all

of the young men eighteen or over were in the service. Only the rejects were left to take care of things on the home front. Some women had parties for the young boys and girls. Most of the women taking part in the games were teaching the young men the facts of life, as these were learning parties. You had to learn the games. "Spin the Bottle" and "Post Office" were the best and most often played. One woman had a party about every month.

This was April and "Party Month." Two young men had attended the party. Since they were tired and sleepy, they headed for home. Having a four-mile walk was not a problem back in the forties. Everyone walked everywhere they went. David and Paul were about halfway home when a spring storm fell on them with full force. As they were in front of the old Eggins house, they decided to go inside until the rain stopped. The rain didn't stop as the two young men stood looking out the window at the storm. The room had three windows, and David was at the middle window. As the lightning flashed, David saw what he thought was Paul, standing and looking out the window on his right. David said, "Boy, this is some storm, isn't it?"

Paul said, "It sure is!" . . . only Paul was standing on David's left when he answered.

David looked around quickly saying, "How did you get over there so quick?"

Paul said, "I haven't moved from this window."

The window on David's right was small and the one of the left was a larger one. David looked over at Paul for a few seconds. It was pitch dark, only the lightning flashes would light up the room some. Paul decided to come over and look out the small window.

David looked at what he thought was Paul standing on his left looking out the big window and said, "I sure wish I was home, don't you?"

Paul said, "I sure do,". . . only Paul was on David's right at the small window. David whirled around so quickly, he hurt his neck and said, "I don't know how you are moving so fast. I just saw you over at the other window."

Paul said, "You never saw me over there! I have been right here." David had a word he always used when he wanted to make a point: Son. He said, "Son, someone is in here with us and I don't like this place anyway. I'm out of here, storm or no storm."

Paul said, "I'm with you."

In a flash, almost as fast as a big lightning flash, they were on their way home. Word soon spread around that the old house was no place to go on a stormy night. A man got the farm for a song and sang it himself. The first thing he did was burn the old house down. People wondered if he had anything to do with ghostly hauntings of the old Eggins house.

Crosby's Old House

Each and every road has a name around here. Some are named after a person or some just have a number, that being the case of this story. The road and hollow are known around here as 5 and 20.

There was a man by the name of Crosby that lived on 5 and 20. He was a very smart fellow, liked by about everyone. He taught school for a living.

Crosby had a very nice family, three girls and one boy. His two youngest girls were the prettiest girls around at that time. All of the boys wanted to date them. Some got to walk the girls home from church now and then, but a lot of the boys never got that lucky.

The girls soon were both married, leaving home to make their living in Columbus, Ohio, leaving Crosby by himself as his wife had passed on, making Crosby a very lonely man.

Crosby lived for about a year after the girls left home. He never went anywhere, or visited his friends or neighbors. He just wasted away. He died alone, being found about two days later by one of his neighbors.

The old house stood empty for a long time. A lot of people said you could hear a very loud noise coming from the house sometimes late at night.

There was a man I will just call N.B. who said he was going home one night after visiting his girlfriend. As he got near the house, the horse he was riding just balked, not wanting to go past the house. After some coaxing, N.B. got the horse to move. Just as he was in front of the house, he said he heard a noise come from within that made his hair stand up. The noise was like nothing he had ever heard before.

The horse broke into a run full speed, going all the way home with N.B. holding on for dear life.

When the horse reached the barn, he was still scared to death. He ran in the barn with N.B. still in the saddle for just a few seconds. The barn door was very low, just reaching above the horse's back. The horse got his rider and saddle off at the same time.

This tale was told many times through the community—some believed it, some didn't.

I bought the old farmhouse back in the late seventies. The only thing I ever saw or heard was just noises most houses make settling.

I sold the place a few years later to a couple that could not stand the noises. They had the house torn down. That was the end of the noise in the old Crosby house.

Sean's Vacation

Sean was telling me about his vacation that he and two of his friends took to Myrtle Beach, South Carolina.

They rented a nice beach house and were having a great time, playing in the ocean and walking and running on the beach.

They went back to the beach house and ate dinner, then his friends decided to go sightseeing. Sean told them to go ahead, he was tired and just wanted to take a nap.

His friends were soon on their way, leaving Sean alone in the big, old house. As he got ready for his nap, he noticed how quiet the house had become.

As he was lying across the bed, he suddenly had a feeling come over him, like he could not move. All at once, something started to smother him. Whatever was doing this was too strong for Sean and he was about to pass out. Sean, being a Christian boy, called out in a loud voice to the One he knew could help him. He asked Jesus to please help him, and said, "In the name of Jesus, release me."

When he spoke the name of Jesus, the smothering stopped and Sean could breathe again. He said he saw nothing except a pillow all wrinkled up. It had been used to smother him.

I wonder if Sean had not called for help from the one he puts his trust in, our Lord and Savior, Jesus Christ, what his friends would have seen when they came back from seeing the sights.

Soft Music

This story was told to me by a very good friend of mine who is a Preacher. . . not one to tell tall tales or lie about things.

At the time, Herman and his wife lived on Ninth Avenue in Huntington, West Virginia. The house they lived in had belonged to an old woman and she had lived there for many years.

She loved to listen to classical music, which she did almost every day. As she grew old and feeble, she sat in one place most of the time and listened to her music that she loved. That is the place she died, doing what she loved so much.

Years later, Herman and his wife bought the house and they also like the place very well.

One day, Herman's Mrs. moved her chair to the same spot where the old woman was sitting on the day she died. The house was quiet and she sat down to relax a bit. Soon she started hearing soft beautiful music. It was relaxing and she closed her eyes, soon falling asleep.

Now, Herman made more noise than a mule in a tin barn. He came in from work making enough noise to raise the dead. As his wife woke from her very relaxing nap, she could still hear the soft music. She asked Herman if he liked that kind of music.

"What kind of music are you talking about?" Herman asked. "I don't hear any music."

His wife said, "You must be deaf. It is loud and clear."

Herman walked over to where his wife was sitting and as he came closer, he could hear the music. He stepped back and the music stopped. As he would go back to his chair, he could hear it still playing. There was only about a four-foot circle where the music could be heard.

Soon after, Herman sold the house. It didn't take him long to sell it after the music started playing.

The Cat

This story is about a good friend of mine and his wife, who is also a good friend.

Todd was a fellow that loved his beer very much. In fact, he was an alcoholic. Every day, he would drive to the store about five miles from his house. He would take his beer home to drink. No one was there except himself, as he was retired, and his wife still worked.

The had moved from town to a small farm with a few acres. They had chickens, pigs, sheep, and calves on the farm that Todd liked to take care of and he did this very well until he got sick.

As time went on, he got worse and was soon bedfast. They had a daughter that took care of him while his wife worked.

Todd was not a religious man, but as he became sicker, he began to have different thoughts about things. Upon hearing this, I called his wife to see if our Pastor and another friend could come with me to pay him a visit to talk to him about accepting Christ into his heart before it was too late. His wife said, "Yes, please come and talk to him."

My Pastor, my friend and I made plans and went to see him. We had a long talk with him about his soul and what it is like to die lost. With tears in his eyes, he rejected the Lord, and said for us to come back the next day so he could have time to think about it. Pastor Moore told him it was a bad decision to put it off by waiting until tomorrow. It was lunchtime when we last saw Todd.

I will never forget the look on his face as we left, not knowing if it would be the last time we would see him alive. About six p.m. that day he died. How sad for me to see a friend die lost. I have always felt I should have done more than I did for Todd that day.

About a year later, I saw Todd's wife at a funeral of another friend. She told me she wanted to share with me something about the day Todd died.

She said that after we left that day, a pretty bird came and sat on the windowsill, pecking on the window. Every now and then it would fly away, come back, and peck on the window again.

Todd watched the bird as it pecked on the glass. He told his wife how pretty the bird was and that he had never seen one like it before. This went on from about one o'clock until about five o'clock, and then the bird flew away. Todd waited for the bird to come back; it never did. About six o'clock that evening, as Todd was looking out the window, a very strange looking cat appeared. It stared at Todd with eyes that looked very evil.

For some reason, not known to Todd's wife, she saw the strange cat also. Todd let out a fearful scream as he looked at the cat. This was the last thing he saw as his breathing ceased and his heart quit beating. His wife quickly called 911.

When the emergency crew arrived, Todd's wife stepped out on the porch. While standing there, she saw the evil-eyed cat as it walked across her yard. It was staring at her as it left, never to be seen again.

Could it be the little bird was an angel sent from above, trying to get Todd to accept Jesus as his Savior before it was too late? Could it be that the evil-looking cat was one of Satan's demons? Todd's wife seemed to think so.

The Man in the Big Chair

This story is about a miracle that is hard for even the doctors to believe.

There was a young man by the name of Van. He was a guy that liked to take a drink of whiskey, smoke pot, and do hard drugs. He was a very kind-hearted young man but had a few bad habits he could not overcome, as a lot of us do.

I do not like to judge people because I have a mirror that reminds me of who that fellow is looking back at me. . . that has not been perfect.

One day, Van got hold of some bad drugs. He was found by his parents, lying by the road, still breathing but very weak. He had vomited and the drugs had badly damaged his lungs. The parents took him to the hospital. They were told that he could not possibly make it, due to the damage to his lungs. The family was very upset, especially his Aunt Sis. She was close to him and a good Christian lady that had many prayers answered. She was a nurse and had seen a lot of bad sickness happen to people as she worked her job. An uncle that also was close to Van asked all of the family to go to the Chapel and pray. They all did as he asked, and asked God for his healing and comfort.

Every morning Sis would wake early and go

see Van on her way to work, taking the nurses doughnuts, fruit and snacks. One morning, she stopped to see him and left feeling very sad about his condition. After she left, a minister named Bob came to see Van and had prayer with him. As soon as he left, Van broke the leather straps on his wrists. The doctors and nurses could not believe his strength.

Sis was unaware of all of this and she drove to work, sad and tearful in prayer, thinking of his parents, brothers and sisters. She passed through Spring Valley on her way to the Veterans' Hospital. It was a dark morning but as she turned the curve at the golf course, she looked up to see bright beams of sunlight shining through the clouds, the rays reaching the ground.

All at once a big man sitting in a large ladder back armchair, his arms on the chair arms, appeared in the middle of the lights shining down. He had a white beard and hair, a snow-white robe and a kind, gentle face and smile. He was chuckling and his body was slightly shaking as he laughed. He said, in a soft reassuring voice, "You don't think I can do it, do you?" With a smile on his face, he and the chair vanished.

This was only a few seconds. Sis was shocked to see what she had just seen. She had a calm feeling that her prayers were answered and they were because that is when the leathers were broken and he didn't have to have them again.

When Van's parents came in, they could not believe that instead of a gravely ill or dead son, they found him alert, awake, and talking. The doctors were as shocked as anyone.

Yes, there is power in prayer and faith.

Van is still living, still kind-hearted and on this

earth for a reason. He will be used as God gives him a mission to tell others about His love.

Does Sis believe she saw God? No, but she knows she saw one of His angels!

Troubled Man

A few years ago, Mr. S. bought a farm adjoining mine and sold it off in lots. There are nice houses on most of the lots. One of the lots was bought by Mr. N. and he was retired and quite different. He bought a very good lot that had a small bench below the level part on top. Not steep at all. It could be worked with a tractor. When Mr. N. took possession, things started to change. He had a big dozer come in to do the work he wanted to fix it the way he wanted it to look.

Soon the level was dozed over the hill, making a big pile of loose dirt. Now it didn't look how Mr. N. wanted it to look, so he had it pushed back up the hill, making it part level and part steep.

Soon Mr. N. started his new dream home. He hired a crew of men that saw how he was and started to take advantage of him. The crew of men worked for over a year on a job that could have been done in ninety days. This cost Mr. N. a large amount of money. They saw he was running out of money and finally finished the job.

Soon Mr. and Mrs. N. moved in their new house. She was working and things seemed normal for about a year or so, until one day it all came to an end. Mr. N. was found shot in the head with a shotgun. He was in the bedroom with his gun beside him.

The Sheriff was soon on the scene to investigate the shooting. Everyone knows they couldn't solve a 3-piece jigsaw puzzle, let alone a crime. It was ruled a suicide.

As time went on, Mrs. N. sold the house to a man who knew nothing about the death of the man in the house. He had never seen a picture and knew nothing about the man who died there.

While Mr. N. was living, he had a fireplace built in the house that was never used. One day the new owner, Mr. D., stopped to talk to me as I was cutting firewood. He is a good religious person and not someone to make things up. He said, "I have never seen a picture of Mr. N., but I can tell you what he looks like."

He proceeded to describe Mr. N., and did very well. I asked, "How do you know what he looked like, if you haven't seen him or a picture of him?"

He said, "A few days ago, I decided to build a fire in the fireplace for the first time." The fireplace worked very well and he had a good fire going in no time. He said he went to the garage to take off his work shoes and coat. When he came back to the living room, there sat Mr. N. in front of the fireplace. He looked around at Mr. D. for a few seconds and just vanished, later to reappear in the kitchen three or four times.

Now, I'm wondering: is Mr. N.'s spirit still in the house he loved so much? If not, what did Mr. D. see?

The Nurse's Light

This story was told to me by a nurse that was with a family the night the light was seen. Another nurse was leaving the home at shift change, and she saw it also.

The two nurses worked for Hospice in the home, caring for people that had only a short time to live. I won't use any names because of the jobs they do, and I'll just call them the two nurses.

They were working at a home in Lincoln County, the last place at the end of a long hollow.

As the evening nurse was leaving, she saw a light coming up the narrow road. It was moving pretty fast, so the nurse decided to wait and see if it was maybe some of the patient's family coming to the house. The nurses were standing on the porch waiting for the visitors to get there. The light came faster. It was about the size of a basketball. When it got to the yard, it just went out.

The evening nurse said to the midnight nurse, "I don't know what we just saw, but I'm glad my shift is over, and I'll be glad to get out of this hollow." She left in a hurry. It was about 12:30 when she left for home.

The midnight nurse went to check on the old gentleman she was to care for and found he was dead. She ran to the door to see if the other nurse was gone and her car was not there. She started back to the old man's room, and as she turned, she saw two glowing lights shoot across the yard, and then down the road the way the one light had come.

Had someone come for the old man? No one knows.

Some other family members came up the hollow in a few minutes and they had very startled looks to their faces. They said that from one end of the hollow to the other, there were little angels hanging on strings, and that it was an unbelievable sight to see. The old man's kind and gentle wife was comforted by the sightings of the lights and angels.

The Burning Stump

Back when I was a young man, I liked to coon hunt. I loved hearing the dogs run and tree a coon. Sometimes, I would one out to see a good fight.

One night, I picked up Jimmy, who hunted with me every weekend, and we talked about where to go hunting that night. We decided to go over on Fees Branch. I had a good friend or two that owned farms over there and they let me hunt on the farms.

After turning the dogs loose, they soon struck a coon—running it down a short distance then up a very steep hill. I don't know why, but a coon always makes it as hard on you as they can. The dogs were soon on top of the hill, then over in the next holler where they treed. Not a prettier sound could be heard.

As we started up the hill, we saw what looked like a light that a fire would make. It was in the path where we were walking. After taking a short rest, we decided to see who was up there with that light. As we got closer, I turned my spotlight on, shining the beam of light on the light in the path, but nothing was there. I turned my spotlight off, quite puzzled, only to have the light reappear. We were walking toward the light all the time and were within fifty feet of it. I turned my spotlight on, only to find nothing there again—only a big old stump. I turned my spotlight off again and the glow reappeared.

I started to feel like Moses and the Burning Bush. As we got closer with our waking light, the glow went out. We both looked the stump over, but found nothing.

I have heard old timers talk of foxfire, so I guess that is what we saw, but I never could figure out why the light never came back on.

When we walked on toward the dogs, after seeing the coon, we tied the dogs up and led them back the same path, but the light never came back on at that stump.

I wonder why?

Two Young Coon Hunters

This tale took place in Bear Hollow, which is located in Mason County, West Virginia, near the Cabell county line. The year was about 2002.

My friend Jim told me about the two young boys that saw the unexplained creature. The two boys were Jim's nephews.

The month of May that year was quite nice. Not much was going on around this part of the county. Hunting season was not in, but you could train your dogs at night if you did not kill the coon. A lot of young men hunted back then. Not as many now, due to housing developments, farms being split up, ground posted, and no good areas to run the dogs. In earlier years, people were allowed to hunt about anywhere around here. . . but it has all changed.

One Friday night, Jim's nephews came to his house to ask about taking his two coonhounds hunting that night. Jim was glad to let the two boys take the dogs hunting. He knew the dogs needed some exercise and he was too lazy to take them himself that evening.

The two dogs' names were Duke and Pup. Old Duke was good, but he couldn't hold Old Pup a light when it comes to treeing coons. Old Pup was getting old, about nine, to be exact. We always wondered why

Jim never called him by any other name. Just Old Pup. It was decided by a few hunters around, that Jim was just too lazy to name his dog. He got him as a pup, and a pup he would stay.

The two boys turned the dogs loose that night in a hollow we all call D.A., which empties into Bear Hollow. All of the side hollows have names. Most got their names from someone that owned the farms the hollows were in.

They had walked more than a hundred yards when they heard Old Duke open up on a track. Old Duke would run anything that made a track, whether it was large or small. Most hunters around called Duke a big game dog because he liked to run deer so much. We all had a lot of fun after any of us would be out hunting—all calling each other to see who could tell the biggest tale about it. We had a lot of fun teasing each other.

But this time, Duke was not running off undesirable game. The two boys knew as soon as Old Pup barked that they had a coon on the run. The chase was fast and short—about one-half mile—when Old Pup let the boys know the chase was over. He had a tree bark you could tell, as soon as he looked up a tree. Old Duke joined in. Both dogs let the world know that Mr. Coon was up that tree.

The dogs had run the coon up the hill, then out to the end of a big flat field, where a row of trees crossed. This led over to another hollow that had a lot of hollow trees in it. The coon didn't know the speed of Old Duke, as he got his speed from running deer. He was a very fast dog.

The two young hunters climbed up the hill in no time at all. When they reached the top, they could tell the dogs were straight ahead. There was another row of trees with a fence nailed on them between the boys and the dogs. Both boys had good spotlights that would reach out a long way. They used their walking lights until they got near the row of trees. One of the boys turned on his spotlight. Standing in the fencerow straight ahead, they saw something that brought them to a halt.

Both boys described the thing as being eight feet tall, with black hair all over and large bright green eyes. It stood there looking directly at the light but never moved. The two boys both showed it how moving was done. They set a new world's record going back to the truck.

They decided to get Jim to come back with them. One of the boys said he would not go back unless Jim took his deer gun. They didn't have to twist Jim's arm very hard to get him to take it along.

Jim, being too lazy to climb the big hill, went in another way. He could drive very close to the dogs the way he went in. When he stopped the truck, he was about one hundred yards from the dogs. Jim had his deer gun in his hands and headed toward the dogs with both the boys right on his heels. Soon they reached the tree where the dogs were. Shining their lights up the tree, they saw the coon looking at them.

They put the leash on the dogs and led them to the spot where the big hairy creature had been standing. It was no longer there. Jim said, "Let Old Duke loose, he will run anything that makes a track. We will find out what you boys saw."

One of the boys led Old Duke over to where the creature had been standing and turned him loose. Old Duke took a sniff. His hair stood up so high, he looked

62

like a porcupine. He turned and headed to the truck like a streak. When he jumped in the truck, he hit his head on the top of the dog box so hard that Jim and the boys could hear it from where they were standing. After hearing Old Duke hit his head, Jim and the boys made a dash for the truck also. Old Duke was a big game dog, but not that big.

No one ever knew what the boys saw that night. Whatever it was, it took the coon hunting out of them. They quit!

Jim no longer hunts, as Old Pup and Duke have passed on to the big green pasture in the sky.

No one hunts the D.A. hollow anymore. I wonder why?

A Place Where the Grass Won't Grow

This story is true—about Mr. Gray and his daughter, Pearl.

Mr. Gray was married to a woman that wouldn't take care of their daughters. During World War II he went into the military service. The wife dropped the girls off at his mother's house and said, "You can have them."

After the war was over, one of the daughters, Pearl, wanted to live with her dad and his new wife. The new wife had two children of her own, very young, about four and six years old. Pearl wasn't much older herself, maybe close to being a teenager.

Mr. Gray and his new wife soon had three children, two boys and one girl. The had a small house and it was pretty crowded. The wife's son left to live with his dad, so there were now only five children left at home. Pearl's sister that had been left at her grandmother's remained there.

Mr. Gray and his wife had a drinking problem. Many nights Pearl was left home to babysit the younger children. She was like a mother to them.

When Pearl was old enough, she married a man that Mr. Gray did not like at all. Being her dad, he wanted to do what was right by her. He gave her a nice place to build a house, and she and her husband started working on it. They both worked hard, as that is all they had both done since they were children. The house was very nice.

Mr. Gray and his son-in-law never got along at all. Pearl would take her husband's side against her dad. This made Mr. Gray very angry. One day he lost his temper telling Pearl, "I hope there will never be grass growing around your house as long as you live."

She and her dad never got along after that.

Soon Mr. Gray's second wife died. All of the children were grown and gone, leaving Mr. Gray alone. He had to drive by Pearl's house every day, and she would turn her head and never speak to him. It hurt him very much. He had quit drinking, attended church and was doing his best, but Pearl never had a good word to say about him. She never checked on him, just let him be. This continued about four years.

Mr. Gray met another woman and married her, but this was not to be. After the ceremony, he died of a heart attack—died before he got to the hospital.

Time passed as usual. After Mr. Gray died, his old house just stood there. Pearl could see it every day.

About a month after Mr. Gray died, Pearl decided to go to the old place to have a look around. As she came to the old house, it felt strange to be there again. As she walked across the porch and started to open the door, she suddenly heard a very loud noise from inside the house. It sounded like someone was kicking the walls out of the house.

Pearl ran from the place. Since she was alone, it really scared her. She looked back over her shoulder and went as fast as she could run.

Pearl and her husband had separated earlier, and as her own children were grown, she lived alone.

She was very shaken up by the noise, but a few days passed, and she felt better and decided to go visit the old house again. As before, she started to open the door and the same noise was heard. It sounded like someone was tearing the house down. Pearl ran away and never went back there again.

It is strange that no one else ever heard the noise but Pearl. The house has been lived in four or five times in the past twenty years, but no one has heard the noise except Pearl.

When Mr. Gray and Pearl had the argument, and he told her he hoped the grass wouldn't grow in her yard, his wish came true. The grass grows up to the edge of the yard, leaving the rest of it as bare as can be.

No grass has grown in the yard since Mr. Gray died.

A Man Called Goat

Back in the late forties or early fifties, not too much went on around here. Most everyone was as poor as a church mouse, and didn't even know it, having very little to speak of, but most had food on the table.

We had a young man in the community that everyone called "Goat" because he bought a goat at the market one day, hauling it home in the back seat of his car. The old goat chewed the seat to pieces. Everyone thought it was funny so the young man got the name Goat.

One day Goat was stopped by the State Police. Goat had the same old car he had hauled the goat home in. Goat was always working on the old car. I guess the policeman wanted to show that he was in charge, as most do. He walked up to the car telling Goat to turn on his lights, which Goat did. However, no light came on. The cop asked, "Where are your lights?"

Goat was quick to reply, "Out on the front porch."

The cop then said, "Will you pull the emergency brake?"

Goat did as he was told, but he had no brake.

The cop then asked, "Where is your emergency brake?"

Goat was quick to answer, "In the back seat."

Now the cop was getting quite fed up with Goat, and his car, and he said, "Will you show me your license plate? It's not on the car, where is it?"

Goat then answered, "At home under the bed."

The cop told him to get the car home and fix it up before he gave him a ticket.

Goat said, "I don't need a ticket. I can't read what it says, anyway."

Hearing this, the cop got in his car, gave it the gas, and covered Goat with gravel as he pulled out. Goat said, "If that man could read, someone ought to give him a ticket for driving that way."

Everyone liked Goat. He was quite a funny man.

One day he was working for a man that ran a store near where he lived. A dark cloud moved in, and Goat was quick to ask the man who ran the store if he could go home before the storm hit. The storekeeper said, "We will be working inside, you won't get wet."

Goat said, "You don't understand. . . Nancy is afraid of thunder and lightning, but I'm not afraid of nothing." (His wife's name was Nancy.)

A few days later, Goat was working for the storekeeper again. He was working on a nearby farm the man owned. It was said back then that sometimes you could see a woman floating near the old house. Some said she floated about four feet off the ground. Goat said he saw the woman floating past him, and he ran home as fast as he could, not stopping at the store as he went by. He had it in high gear. His hair was standing back, and his legs were going ninety miles per hour as he passed the store.

The storekeeper saw Goat the next day, and asked him what his hurry was the evening before. Goat told him he had seen the floating woman. The storekeeper laughed and said, "I thought you said the other day that you wasn't afraid of nothing."

Goat was quick to reply, "I'm not afraid of nothing, but that was something, and I am afraid of something."

Lil's Gramma

Back in the 1930s, times were hard. Most people were good, caring, and hard working. But not all. There was a bad apple or two in every barrel, just like today. Only today, we have a lot more barrels, and a lot more kinds of apples, as the saying goes.

There were a couple of nice people by the name of Bias. They were twin girls. Both girls were married and had families of their own. One lady had seven children, while the other had only one. Her name was Lil.

Now, Gramma Bias had eight grandchildren, and Lil was her favorite. She would play games with Lil, take walks, and do things that little girls like to do. One special treat was eating ice cream. Most every Saturday, she had saved a nickel, and would take Lil to the drug store for an ice cream cone. This went on for about six years. Soon it was time for Lil to start school. She would always stop by Gramma's house on the way home from school.

One day, Lil came running home from school, and she noticed a bunch of people standing on Gramma's porch. One of the women had to tell Lil that her Gramma Bias was dead. What a shock for a little girl.

Two days later, Lil saw her Gramma at the gravesite for the last time—so she thought.

70

About a month later, on a Saturday morning, Lil was going to be able to sleep late, since there was no school. To her surprise, she was awaked from a deep sleep by—who else?—Gramma Bias. She stood by the bed for a few seconds, then spoke to Lil in a soft voice with a look of disappointment, saying, "Lil, they don't have any ice cream here." She faded from sight, never to be seen again by her favorite grandchild, Lil.

Preacher Mike

A few years back, a church out in the country near where I lived was without a preacher. After a few "wannabe" preachers tried out for the job, the church was out to get the best of the lot. As far as I am concerned, they did. His name was Preacher Mike.

Preacher Mike had a young wife at the time. She didn't stay long as the country folks were not in her class. She left for parts unknown.

Preacher Mike, not being a rich man, bought a new mobile home to live in. He decided it would be good to set it by the church, so he could take care of the church and mow the grass when needed.

There is a pretty large cemetery by the church. Preacher Mike had his home set only about fifty feet from it.

Now, some of us men started to tease Mike about that, saying that he would probably have ghosts paying him a visit.

Soon after Preacher Mike moved in his home, some people had a death in their family. Without getting permission from the church leaders, they buried their loved one just in back of the church, very near Preacher Mike's home. Soon things started to happen around the mobile home and also in the church.

Preacher Mike was a very witty man. One of the

men said that all of the men should get together and dig up the man from that grave and move him to the cemetery, out of the church's back yard.

Preacher Mike said he had a better idea. He said, "Let's just move the headstone over there—it wouldn't be as much work." He was kidding, of course.

One day Preacher Mike said he was hearing doors close in the church as he was cleaning it, but no one could be found. He had left the side doors locked, and no one could get in without his seeing them. He said this went on every time he cleaned the church.

Now, preacher Mike was not afraid of ghosts. He said he didn't think about such things. He soon changed his mind.

One day, he was having his morning cup of coffee and someone came to the door, wanting to talk to him. Preacher Mike set his cup down on the coffee table, and went outside to talk with the man. When he came back in the house to pick up his coffee cup, it was not where he had left it. He found it in the sink still half full of coffee. Now, Preacher Mike was sure he had left the cup on the coffee table.

The next day he was drinking his morning coffee as usual, before mowing the lawn at the church. He thought about the day before, when the cup had been in the sink. He decided to leave the coffee cup in the same place, half full of coffee, like it was the day before. He set the cup down on the coffee table and then went out to mow the lawn. He locked the door when he left, to make sure no one could get in while he was going about his work.

Soon his grass-mowing job was finished. He unlocked the door of the house and to his surprise, the cup was in the sink again with the coffee still in it, just like the day before. He said it didn't scare him much.

With the help of a few people in the community, the sounds in the church, and the coffee cup moving every time he went outside, Preacher Mike decided it was time to move on. Some of us hated to see him go. He was probably the best preacher the church ever had.

Her Favorite Son

I had a very good friend I'll call Betty. She was a very good woman. She was liked by everyone that knew her. She taught school for many years. All of the children in her class each year only had good things to say about her.

Betty had three sons, as many women do. She had a favorite one: the middle one.

While she was living, Betty was a member at the church my wife and I attended. Each year, when she had pears on her tree, she would give them to us to can. We would visit her quite often, just to talk. She liked for us to come for a visit.

She lost her husband a few years back, which made her closer to the boys. The middle son looked and acted like his dad.

As time went on, the middle son married a girl he had known for a long time. She was a very nice girl from a good family. But that wasn't good enough for Betty. As she saw it, no girl was good enough for her favorite son.

As time went on, the son started drinking and gambling, and he liked to play the dog track. You could find him there quite often.

He had a heart attack one day as he was coming home from the dog track. He was found dead at the side of the road. His truck was pulled off the road before he died.

Betty never did get over losing her favorite son. She spoke of him as if he were still alive.

One day my wife and I stopped to see Betty. When she came to the door, she was crying. I felt sorry for her but said nothing. She asked us to sit down, which we did. She wiped the tears from her eyes, saying that she had just had an argument with her son over his wife. I thought she was talking about her youngest son who lived near her. I had just driven past his house and he was working in the fields with the tractor. I said to Betty that her youngest son looked like he was glad to see us come for a visit.

Betty said it wasn't her youngest son, it was the middle son. I said that I hadn't seen her middle son as we came in. At this, Betty said, "He always leaves out the back way when anyone comes in. He comes to visit every day and we have argued over his wife."

Now, I wonder why and how often she saw her son. She was forgetful but very intelligent.

Betty is gone now. She passed away a few years back. She was a good friend and a good Christian, the kind every community needs more of. We miss her very much. I guess being forgetful had given her a lot of comfort, as she saw her son and seemed to be living in the past.

The Old Arnett Church

When I was a young man, or boy, as some would say, I was like most boys when it came to girls. I went to school with a young girl who had red hair. I thought she was the girl of my dreams. I have been told by a friend of mine that a red-headed woman is like a red horse: you can't do much with them, as they have a head of their own.

One day at school, the young girl said that she would be at the church that night down on Guyan Creek. The church was five miles from where I lived. Not having any other way to get there but walk— walk I did.

About halfway to the church, I had to pass an old, run down church house that had not been used for years. The road went right in front of the old Arnett Church. I didn't think anything about the old church or the long walk I had in front of me. I just kept walking.

Soon I got to the Guyan Creek Church. I walked in and found a seat. I looked around for the redhead, but she wasn't to be seen. I sat there for about an hour. I saw that I had been stood up, so I got up, leaving the church before the service was over. It was dark and I had a long walk, with no light to walk by.

I walked at a pace I can't run now. I soon came

to the old church, and boy, was I surprised to hear singing coming from inside. I thought about running past the church and not stopping, but, not being very smart, I looked in the church—only to see a lantern sitting on the old altar, with a man having service by himself. I stood in the dark a little while before saying anything.

When I asked the man what he was doing, it scared the poor fellow more than he had scared me. I knew the man but he didn't know me. He always had about half a load, or as some would say, half a bubble off center.

After talking to the man a few minutes, I started on home. Only having two miles to go, I decided to kick it in high gear. I set a new world record from Arnett Church to home that hasn't been broken to this day.

Aren't young men funny at times, especially in the springtime? A few people who had heard the singing in the old church—before I found out who was doing it—were sure relieved to know the old church wasn't haunted like they thought it was.

It had been going on for about six months. No one had the nerve to see what was going on. I had no other choice.

The Last Goodbye

This story took place near Point Pleasant, West Virginia. I know the man very well. He was not a man to make up stories. His name was Carl and his friend was Elmer.

They lived close to each other and both liked to coon hunt. The always tried to outdo each other with their dogs.

Elmer never had a very good dog; he usually had a plunker. On the other hand, Carl always had a good dog. If it wasn't a good coon dog, he didn't keep it long. Every coon hunter in that part of the country liked to hunt with Carl and is outstanding dogs. Elmer was no exception.

Carl and Elmer lived two very different lifestyles. Elmer was a preacher and Carl a trader that also liked to drink.

Elmer always talked to Carl about the life he was living, and would witness to Carl about the Lord every chance he got.

Carl's health started to fail him. He knew he didn't have long to live. He accepted Christ into his life as many do when they see the end in sight. Some never do; they are just wood for the Devil's fire.

Just like one old woman in a nursing home did. She had a very foul mouth, always saying bad things to people, and not a believer by any means. One day the nursing staff heard her screaming at the top of her voice, saying, "Don't put me in that fire." She just kept repeating, "Don't put me in that fire."

The nurses ran to her room to see what was wrong and she was dying. A very sad ending to the life she had lived—but evidently she waited too long.

Now Carl had a wife that he loved very much, and everyone thought she would outlive Carl, but this was not to be. She was found dead one day as she took a nap on the couch.

Carl was heartbroken. He had lost the love of his life. The day of the funeral was hard for him, but he made it through. That night Carl went to bed and saw something that he later told Elmer about.

He said as he was lying in bed, that all at once a small red light appeared in the room. It circled the room three times, shining on the wall. The light was about the size of a golf ball.

Elmer asked Carl if he had started drinking again. Carl said, "I have not had a drink of any kind, not even coffee!"

Carl is gone now. He has gone to be with his wife in the hereafter.

What was the light that Carl saw? Was it his wife's spirit coming to say goodbye? No one living will know, but I'll bet Carl does!

The Crossing

A nurse by the name of Marty was working with a young man called Dan. He was about 29 years old and dying of AIDS. Dan was good-hearted, always the peacemaker, and helping people.

One day as Marty was doing some of Dan's care, she asked if he was saved. He laughed and said, "I used to be an atheist, but since being so sick, I am now agnostic."

As his condition became worse, and he was very weak and nearing death, Marty explained to his family that as people die, they sometimes need permission from their loved ones to die a peaceful death. She encouraged the dad and mom to let him know it would be okay, and that he could let go.

Dan continued to weaken and would jibber-jabber in his speech, making it very difficult to understand. Marty was becoming somewhat irritated, to say the least, at the way they were not talking to him about dying. He seemed to need them to, especially his mother.

Finally Dan began talking about seeing a bridge and was asking if just anyone could go on it. Marty did not feel it was her place to do so, but finally told him anyone could go on the bridge.

His dad was listening as Marty and Dan talked.

Don asked in broken speech, "If I was black, could I go on the bridge?"

Marty kept assuring him, "Yes, anyone could go on the bridge if they were saved."

The dad spoke up and said, "He is talking about the bridge that we crossed down in Florida."

Dan said, "No! No! The causeway not connected to this earth. Can anyone go on it?" He went on to say there were six guards, two at the west gate and four at the causeway.

Marty quietly told him to go on the bridge over the beautiful way and he soon died.

Later the family looked up the word "causeway" and referenced it to the Bible.

Marty still believes Dan had let the family know in his last few minutes on earth that he did not die lost, and was believing in God.

To Shuppim and Hosah [the lot came forth]
westward, with the gate Shallecheth,
by the causeway of the going up, ward against ward.

1 Chronicles 26:16 (KJV)

LaVergne, TN USA
18 January 2010
170298LV00003B/13/P